To Anne
with love from
Medbh
at the Shelbourne
after our wonderful
meal
together.
Please try to get
to Belfast.

M

Gallery Books
Editor: Peter Fallon

SELECTED POEMS

Medbh McGuckian

SELECTED
POEMS

1978-1994

Gallery Books

Selected Poems
is first published
simultaneously in paperback
and in a clothbound edition
on 10 October 1997.

The Gallery Press
Loughcrew
Oldcastle
County Meath
Ireland

ISBN 1 85235 203 5 (*paperback*)
1 85235 204 3 (*clothbound*)

The Gallery Press receives financial assistance from An Chomhairle
Ealaíon / The Arts Council, Ireland, and acknowledges also the assis-
tance of the Arts Council of Northern Ireland.

Contents

for Marie

On Banna Strand

'When I landed in Ireland,' he was to tell his sister in a letter written while he was awaiting execution, 'swamped and swimming ashore on an unknown strand, I was happy for the first time for over a year. Although I knew that this fate waited on me, I was for one brief spell happy and smiling once more. I cannot tell you what I felt. The sandhills were full of skylarks rising in the dawn, the first I had heard for years — the first sound I heard through the surf was their song, as I waded through the breakers, and they kept rising all the time up to the old rath at Currsahone, where I stayed and sent the others on, and all around were primroses and wild violets and the singing of the skylarks in the air, and I was back in Ireland again.'

Roger Casement

Smoke

They set the whins on fire along the road.
I wonder what controls it, can the wind hold
that snake of orange motion to the hills,
away from the houses?

They seem so sure what they can do.
I am unable even
to contain myself, I run
till the fawn smoke settles on the earth.

Faith

My grandmother led us to believe in snow
as an old man in the sky shaking
feathers down from his mattress over the world.

Her bed in the morning was covered with tiny scales,
sloughed off in the night from peeling skin;
they floated in a cloud

of silver husks to the floor, or spun
in the open window like starry litter,
blowing along the road.

I burned them in a heap, a dream of coins
more than Thérèse's promised shower of roses,
or Virgil's souls, many as autumn leaves.

The 'Singer'

In the evenings I used to study
at my mother's old sewing-machine,
pressing my feet occasionally
up and down on the treadle
as though I were going somewhere
I had never been.

Every year at exams, the pressure mounted —
the summer light bent across my pages
like a squinting eye. The children's shouts
echoed the weather of the street,
a car was thunder,
the ticking of a clock was heavy rain . . . .

In the dark I drew the curtains
on young couples stopping in the entry,
heading home. There were nights
I sent the disconnected wheel
spinning madly round and round
till the empty bobbin rattled in its case.

Lychees

You wonder at that Georgian terrace
miles out of town where the motorway begins.
My great-grandfather was a coachman
and knew how far away he was in the dark
by mysteries of the Rosary. My grandmother said
you could tell a good husband
by the thumbed leaves of his prayer-book.

A dead loss, my mother counts you,
setting my teeth on edge at all hours,
getting me to break the lychee's skin.
She underestimates the taste of sacrifice,
the irrelevance of distances,
cat's-eyes, the cleanness of hands.

Slips

The studied poverty of a moon roof,
the earthenware of dairies cooled by apple trees,
the apple tree that makes the whitest wash . . .

But I forget names, remembering them wrongly
where they touch upon another name,
a town in France like a woman's Christian name.

My childhood is preserved as a nation's history,
my favourite fairytales the shells
leased by the hermit crab.

I see my grandmother's death as a piece of ice,
my mother's slimness restored to her,
my own key slotted in your door —

tricks you might guess from this unfastened button,
a pen mislaid, a word misread,
my hair coming down in the middle of a conversation.

Aunts

My aunts jived their way
through the '50s to my teens.
They lay till noon and called me up
to listen for their lovers at the gate,
and paid me for the colour of their eyes —
'Grey,' I said, or 'Brown,' when they wanted
blue or hazel, in their giggling,
sleeping-together dreams.

I watched them shading in their lips
from sugar pink to coral, from mulberry to rose,
and their wet skirts hungry for
the brilliance of their swing,
as they dried by the strange
elastic girdles, paper petticoats.

Once out of the blue
I caught them dancing on the bed,
with their undergrowth of hazel,
and their make-up sweated through.

The Hollywood Bed

We narrow into the house, the room, the bed,
where sleep begins its shunting. You adopt
your mask, your intellectual cradling of the head,
neat as notepaper in your creaseless
envelope of clothes, while I lie crosswise,
imperial as a favoured only child,
calmed by sagas of how we lay like spoons
in a drawer, till you blew open
my tightened bud, my fully-buttoned housecoat,
like some Columbus mastering
the saw-toothed waves, the rows of letter *m*s.

Now the headboard is disturbed
by your uncomfortable skew, your hands
like stubborn adverbs visiting your face,
or your shoulder, in your piquancy of dreams,
the outline that, if you were gone,
would find me in your place.

The Soil-Map

I am not a woman's man, but I can tell,
by the swinging of your two-leaf door,
you are never without one man in the shadow
of another; and because the mind
of a woman between two men is lighter
than a spark, the petalled steps to your porch
feel frigid with a lost warmth. I will not
take you in hardness, for all the dark cage
of my dreaming over your splendid fenestration,
your moulded sills, your slender purlins,

the secret woe of your gutters. I will do it
without niggardliness, like food with one
generous; a moment as auspicious
and dangerous as the christening of a ship,
my going in to find the settlement
of every floor, the hump of water
following the moon, and her discolouring,
the saddling derangement of a roof
that might collapse its steepness
under the sudden strain of clearing its name.

For anyone with patience can divine
how your plasterwork has lost key, the rendering
about to come away. So like a rainbird,
challenged by a charm of goldfinch,
I appeal to the god who fashions edges
whether such turning-points exist
as these saltings we believe we move
away from, as if by simply shaking
a cloak we could disbud ourselves,
dry out, and cease to live there?

I have found the places on the soil-map,
proving it possible once more to call
houses by their names, Annsgift or Mavisbank,
Mount Juliet or Bettysgrove: they should not
lie with the gloom of disputes to interrupt them
every other year, like some disease
of language making humorous the friendship
of the thighs. I drink to you as Hymenstown,
(my touch of fantasy) or First Fruits,
impatient for my power as a bride.

Gateposts

A man will keep a horse for prestige,
but a woman ripens best underground.
He settles where the wind
brings his whirling hat to rest,
and the wind decides which door is to be used.

Under the hip-roofed thatch,
the bed-wing is warmed by the chimney breast;
on either side the keeping-holes
for his belongings, hers.

He says it's unlucky to widen the house
and leaves the gateposts holding up the fairies.
He lays his lazy-beds and burns the river,
he builds turf-castles,
and sprigs the corn with apple-mint.

She spreads heather on the floor
and sifts the oatmeal ark for thin-bread farls:
all through the blue month, July,
she tosses stones in basins to the sun,
and watches for the trout in the holy well.

Matchmaking

The mayflies' opera is their only moon, only
those that fall on water reproduce, content
with scattering in fog or storm, such ivory
as elephants hold lofty, like champagne.

The Flower Master

Like foxgloves in the school of the grass moon
we come to terms with shade, with the principle
of enfolding space. Our scissors in brocade,
we learn the coolness of straight edges, how
to stroke gently the necks of daffodils
and make them throw their heads back to the sun.

We slip the thready stems of violets, delay
the loveliness of the hibiscus dawn with quiet ovals,
spirals of feverfew like water splashing,
the papery legacies of bluebells. We do
sea-fans with sea-lavender, moon-arrangements
roughly for the festival of moon-viewing.

This black container calls for sloes, sweet
sultan, dainty nipplewort, in honour
of a special guest who, summoned to the
tea ceremony, must stoop to our low doorway,
our fontanelle, the trout's dimpled feet.

The Aphrodisiac

She gave it out as if it were
a marriage or a birth, some other
interesting family event, that she
had finished sleeping with him, that
her lover was her friend. It was his heart
she wanted, the bright key to his study,
not the menacings of love. So he is
banished to his estates, to live
like a man in a glasshouse; she has taken to
a little cap of fine white lace
in the mornings, feeds her baby
in a garden you could visit blindfold
for its scent alone:
                    But though a ray of grace
has fallen, all her books seem as frumpish
as the last year's gambling game, when she
would dress in pink taffeta, and drive
a blue phaeton, or in blue, and drive
a pink one, with her black hair supported
by a diamond comb, floating about
without panniers. How his most
caressing look, his husky whisper suffocates her,
this almost perfect power of knowing
more than a kept woman. The between-maid
tells me this is not the only secret staircase.
Rumour has it she's taken to rouge again.

The Flitting

'You wouldn't believe all this house has cost me —
in body-language terms, it has turned me upside down.'
I've been carried from one structure to the other
on a chair of human arms, and liked the feel
of being weightless, that fraternity of clothes . . . .
Now my own life hits me in the throat, the bumps
and cuts of the walls as telling
as the poreholes in strawberries, tomato seeds.
I cover them for safety with these Dutch girls
making lace, or leaning their almond faces
on their fingers with a mandolin, a dreamy
chapelled ease abreast this other turquoise-turbanned,
glancing over her shoulder with parted mouth.

She seems a garden escape in her unconscious
solidarity with darkness, clove-scented
as an orchid taking fifteen years to bloom,
and turning clockwise as the honeysuckle.
Who knows what importance
she attaches to the hours?
Her narrative secretes its own values, as mine might
if I painted the half of me that welcomes death
in a faggotted dress, in a peacock chair,
no falser biography than our casual talk
of losing a virginity, or taking a life, and
no less poignant if dying
should consist in more than waiting.

I postpone my immortality for my children,
little rock-roses, cushioned
in long-flowering sea-thrift and metrics,
lacking elemental memories:

I am well-earthed here as the digital clock,
its numbers flicking into place like overgrown farthings
on a bank where once a train
ploughed like an emperor living out a myth
through the cambered flesh of clover and wild carrot.

Power-Cut

The moon is salmon as a postage-stamp
over the tonsured trees, a rise-and-fall lamp
in a cracked ice ceiling. The cruelty
of road conditions flushes summer near,
as the storm seal hangs along the pier.

My dishes on the draining-board
lie at an even keel, the baby lowered
into his lobster-pot pen; my sponge
disintegrates in water like a bird's nest,
a permanent wave gone west.

These plotted holes of days my keep-net shades,
soluble as refuse in canals; the old flame
of the candle sweats in the night, its hump
a dowager's with bones running thin:
the door-butler lets the rain begin.

The Heiress

You say I should stay out of the low
fields; though my hands love dark,
I should creep till they are heart-shaped,
like Italian rooms no longer hurt by sun.

When I look at the striped marble of the glen,
I see the husbandry of a good spadesman,
lifting without injury, or making sure
where the furrow is this year the ridge
will be the next; and my pinched grain,
hanging like a window on the smooth spot
of a mountain, or a place for fawns, watches
your way with horses, your delicate Adam work.

But I am lighter of a son, through my slashed
sleeves the inner sleeves of purple keep remembering
the moment exactly, remembering the birth
of an heiress means the gobbling of land.

Dead leaves do not necessarily
fall; it is not coldness, but the tree itself
that bids them go, preventing their destruction.
So I walk along the beach, unruly, I drop
among my shrubbery of seaweed my black acorn buttons.

The Difficult Age

He could not leave his own voice alone:
he took it apart, he undressed it,
I suppose the way that women clear their faces,
so that some light is still able to love them.

He had pushed his voice up from his chest
into his head until the air from his lungs
was felt between the eyes. I heard
those curiously distorted flicks of sound

like an English choirboy or coherent father,
or the faraway splash of a brief and dowdy
bird, turning over its final twenty-second held
note. I would bid my memory be emotionless

as the second in which his studied lateness
summoned up an image of sheltered orchids,
guarding in their permanent white premonitions
such easy words as 'Je ne suis pas heureuse'.

To the Nightingale

I remember our first night in this grey
and paunchy house: you were still slightly
in love with me, and dreamed of having
a grown son, your body in the semi-gloom
turning my dead layers into something
resembling a rhyme. That smart and
cheerful rain almost beat the hearing
out of me, and yet I heard my name
pronounced in a whisper as a June day
will force itself into every room.

To the nightingale it made no difference,
of course, that you tossed about an hour,
two hours, till what was left of your future
began; nor to the moon that nearly rotted,
like the twenty-first century growing
its grass through me; but became in the end,
while you were still asleep, a morning
where I saw our neighbours' mirabelle
bent over our hedge, and its trespassing
fruit, unacknowledged as our own.

From the Dressing-Room

Left to itself, they say, every foetus
would turn female, staving in, nature
siding then with the enemy that
delicately mixes up genders. This
is an absence I have passionately sought,
brightening nevertheless my poet's attic
with my steady hands, calling him my blue
lizard till his moans might be heard
at the far end of the garden. For I like
his ways, he's light on his feet and does
not break anything, puts his entire soul
into bringing me a glass of water.

I can take anything now, even his being
away, for it always seems to me his
writing is for me, as I walk springless
from the dressing-room in a sisterly
length of flesh-coloured silk. Oh there
are moments when you think you can
give notice in a jolly, wifely tone,
tossing off a very last and sunsetty
letter of farewell, with strict injunctions
to be careful to procure his own lodgings:
that my good little room is lockable,
but shivery, I recover at the mere
sight of him propping up my pillow.

The Sitting

My half-sister comes to me to be painted:
she is posing furtively, like a letter being
pushed under a door, making a tunnel with her
hands over her dull-rose dress. Yet her coppery
head is as bright as a net of lemons. I am
painting it hair by hair as if she had not
disowned it, or forsaken those unsparkling
eyes as blue may be sifted from the surface
of a cloud; and she questions my brisk
brushwork, the note of positive red
in the kissed mouth I have given her,
as a woman's touch makes curtains blossom
permanently in a house: she calls it
wishfulness, the failure of the tampering rain
to go right into the mountain, she prefers
my sea-studies, and will not sit for me
again, something half-opened, rarer
than railroads, a soiled red-letter day.

On Not Being Your Lover

Your eyes were ever brown, the colour
of time's submissiveness. Love nerves
or a heart beat in their world of
privilege. I had not yet kissed you
on the mouth.

But I would not say, in my un-freedom
I had weakly drifted there, like the
bone-deep blue that visits and decants
the eyes of our children:

How warm and well-spaced their dreams
you can tell from the sleep-late mornings
taken out of my face! Each lighted
window shows me cardiganed, more desolate
than the garden, and more hallowed
than the hinge of the brass-studded
door that we close, and no one opens,
that we open and no one closes.

In a far-flung, too young part,
I remembered all your slender but
persistent volume said, friendly, complex
as the needs of your new and childfree girl.

Isba Song

Beyond the edge of the desk, the Victorian dark
inhabits childhood, youth-seeking, death-seeking,
bringing almost too much meaning to my life,
who might have been content with one storey
and the turned-outwards windows of the isba.
Its mournful locus, I sit like a horse chosen
for its strength, requiring to be renamed
'Monplaisir', with my two hands free. I have heard
in it the sound of another woman's voice,
which I believed was the sound of my own,
the sound the first-timeness of things we remember
must make inside. And although she was eager
to divide her song, from her I took nothing
but the first syllable of her name, so the effect
was of a gentler terrain within a wilder one,
high-lying, hard, as wood might learn to understand
the borrowings of water, or pottery capitulate
its dry colours. Otherwise I might have well
ignored the ground that shone for me, that did enough
to make itself rebound from me, out of which I was made.

Hotel

I think the detectable difference
between winter and summer is a damsel
who requires saving, a heroine half-
asleep and measurably able to hear
but hard to see, like the spaces
between the birds when I turn
back to the sky for another empty feeling.

I would bestow on her a name
with a hundred meanings, all of them
secret, going their own way, as surely
as the silvery mosaic of the previous
week, building itself a sort of hotel
in her voice, to be used whenever
the tale was ruthlessly retold.

And let her learn from the sky, which was
clever and quiet, the rain for its suddenness,
that yes on its own can be a sign for silence,
even from that all-too-inviting mouth.

Dovecote

I built my dovecote all from the same tree
to supplement the winter, and its wood
so widely ringed, alive with knots, reminded me
how a bow unstrung returns again to straight,
how seldom compound bows are truly sweet.

It's like being in a cloud that never rains,
the way they rise above the storm, and sleep
so bird-white in the sky, like day-old
infant roses, little unambitious roads,
islands not defecting, wanting to be rescued.

Since I liked their manners better than
the summer, I kept leaning to the boat-shaped
spirit of my house, whose every room
gives on to a garden, or a sea that knows
you cannot reproduce in your own shade.

Even to the wood of my sunflower chest,
or my kimono rack, I owed no older debt
than to the obligatory palette of the rain
that brought the soil back into tension on my slope
and the sea in, making me an island once again.

Pain Tells You What to Wear

Once you have seen a crocus in the act
of giving way to the night, your life
no longer lives you, from now on
your later is too late. Rain time
and sun time, that red and gold sickness
is like two hands covering your face —
it hardly matters if a whole summer
is ruined by a crumpled piece of paper
or the dry snap of a suitcase closing.

Of all silences, the hardest to bear
is the strange vegetation of your clothes,
a brand-new sleeve becoming haggard
with a garden's thousand adjoining moods.
To make such overperfumed wood speak
a forest language, one must not remember
the mahogany secrecy of eyes once velvet-dark,
now water-pale — the special lighting
of their insolent lying there.

Fear of retouching is the very last
quality suggested by the flag-red,
flag-gold, storming flowers that,
without being seen, like one dissatisfied
with his sirings, reach out through winged
garments to the priceless vertebrae of the stars.

What Does 'Early' Mean?

Happy house across the road,
my eighteen-inch deep study of you
is like a chair carried out into the garden
and back again because the grass is wet.

Yet I think winter has ended
privately in you, and lies in half-sleep,
or her last sleep, at the foot
of one of your mirrors — hence
the spring-day smile with which
you smarten up your mouth
into a retina of new roofs, new thoughts.

None of my doors has slammed
like that. Every sentence is the same
old workshop sentence, ending
rightly or wrongly in the ruins
of an evening spent in puzzling
over the meaning of six o'clock or seven:

Or why the house across the road
has such a moist-day sort of name,
evoking ships and their wind-blown ways.

A Conversation Set to Flowers

That fine china we conceived in spring
and lost in summer has blown the final crumbs
out of the book I was reading; though one
is still bending over prams, an ice-blue peak
over the frills of houses.

The dress of ecru lace you bought me
at the February sales is still all heart.
I cup my hands, thin as a window-pane
unevenly blown, as if to hold
some liquid in my palm, and the rings
slide up and down.

In my birth-dreams light falls in pleats
or steps, the room after those terrible attacks
is a white forest, scented with sea,
and we both change into apples, my breasts
and knees into apples, though you
are more apple than they could possibly be.

But what the snow said, long ago,
to the grey north door and the short day,
breaks through like the multi-coloured
sunrise round a stamp on a letter.
A hill-wind blows at the book's edges
to open a page.

Sea or Sky?

Small doses, effleurage will do,
because I never garden. Wednesday comes
out of the rim of bones with a port-wine
stain on its face, a day of possible
excitements, no sky, yet you know immediately
the colour it should be. I play it down,
the agitated sky of my choice; I assume
that echo of light over there is the sun
improperly burning. In a sea of like mood
a wave is trying to break, to give a reason
for water striking something else, and the grey
below the wave is a darker version
of the moisture-laden sky I should be working in.

The athletic anatomy of waves, in their
reflectiveness, rebirth, means my new, especially
dense breasts can be touched, can be
uplifted from the island of burned skin
where my heart used to be, now I'm
seeing eyes that, sea or sky, have seen you.

Minus 18 Street

I never loved you more
than when I let you sleep another hour,
as if you intended to make such a gate of time
your home. Speechless as night animals,
the breeze and I breakfasted
with the pure desire of speech; but let
each petal of your dream have its chance,
the many little shawls that covered you.

I never envied your child's face
its motherless cheekbones or sensed in them
the approach of illness — how you were being
half-killed on a seashore, or falling
from a ladder where you knelt to watch
the quartering of the moon.

Sleep for you is a trick
of the frost, a light green room in a French house,
giving no trouble till spring.
The wedding-boots of the wind
blow footsteps behind me.
I count each season for the sign
of wasted children.

Sky of blue water, blue-water sky,
I sleep with the dubious kiss
of my sky-blue portfolio.
Under or over the wind,
in soft and independent clothes,
I begin each dawn-coloured picture
deep in your snow.

Querencia

Her hands come awake from the apple-green shutters
of sleep. She clasps the end of her leather belt tightly,
as if she can no longer speak for herself or only
with telephone distortions, the meaning of a row
of black spinal buttons between sender and receiver.

Now here is her favourite cup with its matching plate
and a letter so young, something inside her feels
just like the lines and better than sleep.
As she walks to the window, she smooths out her girlhood
into a shadow of body-colour.

It is strange, how his eyelids close from below,
how love blows her hair to the right, his first beard
to the left. A face in a photograph destroyed
since childhood catches her by the gate-legged
oak table — the chance-seen face like a cold moonstone
in the window's sixteen panes.

She remembers his having to throw stones in the water
to break his dream — and how the river returned them —
or seated at the stone table under the yew, explaining
his need for streets.

At which the birds and vine bed-hangings complain, we have
been taken in too many times by leaves against the window:
a window should be a wide-eaved colour beyond anything.

The Blue She Brings with Her

for Teresa

November — like a man taking all
his shirts, and all his ties, little by little —
enters a million leaves, and that
lion-coloured house-number, the sun,
into his diary; with a rounded symbol —
Nothing — to remind himself of callow apples,
dropping with a sense of rehearsal in June
as if their thought were being done by others.

The mirror bites into me as cloud into
the river-lip of a three-cornered lake
that when the moon is new is shaped
like the moon. With a sudden crash
my log falls to ashes, a wood of winter
colours I have never seen — blood-kissed,
the gold-patterned dishes
show themselves for a moment like wild creatures.

While any smoke that might be going loose
the hot room gathers like a mountain
putting out a mist, and not the kind that clears.
Something you add about mountains makes
my mouth water like a half-lifted cloud
I would choose, if I could, to restrain
as a stone keeps its memories.

Your eyes change colour as you move
and will not go into words. Their swanless
sky-curve holds like a conscious star
a promise from the wind about the blue
she brings with her. If beauty lives
by escaping and leaves a mark, your wrist
will have the mark of my fingers in the morning.

Four O'Clock, Summer Street

As a child cries, all over, I kept insisting
on robin's egg blue tiles about the fireplace,
which gives a room a kind of flying-heartedness.

Only that tiny slice of the house absorbed
my perfume — like a kiss sliding off into
a three-sided mirror — like a red-brown girl

in cuffless trousers we add to ourselves by looking.
She had the boy-girl body of a flower,
moving once and for all past the hermetic front door.

I knew she was drinking blue and it had dried
in her; she carried it wide awake in herself
ever after, and its music blew that other look

to bits. If what she hunted for could fit my eyes,
I would shine in the window of her blood like wine,
or perfume, or till nothing was left of me but listening.

Scenes from a Brothel

Daughters of different mothers may have
the same eyes, but not the same look
in their eyes, for only stone goes well with water.

One has lips so virginal, they seem to be edged
with snow, the discoloured whiteness waiting
within ourselves.
Her teeth are pressed like seeds
against one another, all her bones are armour,
and anything one says reaches the scroll
of her body slowly, her madonna
parting, her milk-fed hands.

I would prefer to be kissed by other
grown-up lips, but her younger sister
speaks with the rapid beating of fish
breathing out of water.
Her face glitters, becoming blurred
like blondes in warm countries.
She stands as though interrupted
in a swift movement, or kissing in flight,
her gown a whirlwind of silk flowers
open to bursting-point.

Any colour lasts a second, three or four
minutes at most — and can never be repeated.
So few words for so many colours.
This blue, this blue, an enfeebled red,
the child of old parents.
Though it is immutable, it has no more lustre
than the moon in its first quarter
or the wall above the coat-stand.

I wish her room were a square bed
with the sheets gushing up like a beautiful
expanse of water. The mirror doubles distances
so the garden is a cascade of paths.
How cold the sea must be,
to make all faces the same!

She lets her arm rest, like the tulip's turn,
on the wheat of her voice. She splashes
the much-caressed sky till its distress
is lighted from the other side.
The silk cracks at its blue corners
as if her bones were the weight and shape of birds'.

The Dream-Language of Fergus

1

Your tongue has spent the night
in its dim sack as the shape of your foot
in its cave. Not the rudiment
of half a vanquished sound,
the excommunicated shadow of a name,
has rumpled the sheets of your mouth.

2

So Latin sleeps, they say, in Russian speech,
so one river inserted into another
becomes a leaping, glistening, splashed
and scattered alphabet
jutting out from the voice,
till what began as a dog's bark
ends with bronze, what began
with honey ends with ice;
as if an aeroplane in full flight
launched a second plane,
the sky is stabbed by their exits
and the mistaken meaning of each.

3

Conversation is as necessary
among these familiar campus trees
as the apartness of torches;
and if I am a threader
of double-stranded words, whose
Quando has grown into now,

no text can return the honey
in its path of light from a jar,
only a seed-fund, a pendulum,
pressing out the diasporic snow.

On Ballycastle Beach

for my father

If I found you wandering round the edge
of a French-born sea, when children
should be taken in by their parents,
I would read these words to you,
like a ship coming in to harbour,
as meaningless and full of meaning
as the homeless flow of life
from room to homesick room.

The words and you would fall asleep,
sheltering just beyond my reach
in a city that has vanished to regain
its language. My words are traps
through which you pick your way
from a damp March to an April date,
or a mid-August misstep; until enough winter
makes you throw your watch, the heartbeat
of everyone present, out into the snow.

My forbidden squares and your small circles
were a book that formed within you
in some pocket, so permanently distended,
that what does not face north faces east.
Your hand, dark as a cedar lane by nature,
grows more and more tired of the skidding light,
the hunched-up waves, and all the wet clothing,
toys and treasures of a late summer house.

Even the Atlantic has begun its breakdown
like a heavy mask thinned out scene after scene
in a more protected time — like one who has

gradually, unnoticed, lengthened her pre-wedding
dress. But, staring at the old escape and release
of the water's speech, faithless to the end,
your voice was the longest I heard in my mind,
although I had forgotten there could be such light.

The Bond

If I use my forbidden hand
to raise a bridge across the river,
all the work of the builders
has been blown up by sunrise.

A boat comes up the river by night
with a woman standing in it,
twin candles lit in her eyes
and two oars in her hands.

She unsheathes a pack of cards.
'Will you play forfeits?' she says.
We play and she beats me hands down,
and she puts three banns upon me:

Not to have two meals in one house,
not to pass two nights under one roof,
not to sleep twice with the same man
until I find her. When I ask her address,

'If it were north I'd tell you south,
if it were east, west.' She hooks
off in a flash of lightning, leaving me
stranded on the bank,

my eyes full of candles,
and the two dead oars.

after the Irish of Nuala Ní Dhomhnaill

The Sun-Moon Child

I dreamt I could make from the summer
a winter childbirth, by turning the slats
of a window to darken a room in Italy.
The house was impossibly fragile, made
of cloth and glass, the room floated freely
within itself, and the bed was let into
a recess, like a stitch that is slack and loose.

My dress was gun-metal grey, with a blow-away
hem: I had saved up my money in an old,
shoulder-length evening glove, and the third
and fifteenth of every month were our first meeting,
our first night. Sleep hammered out the days
within the bounds of an hour; I accepted the dream's
standpoint and decision, like a false season.

His skin and hair and eyes were cloaked
in the warm tones of the day, so he was an Adam
of the young dead of World War One,
or Satan, in the shape of a star-jessamine,
who cursed by name the moon and its perfume.
The clouds had space to travel the grey
background of his seven-minute flame,

until the cherry-spotted bed to the right
of the Spanish Steps became
a blanket of chance-gathered roses
for Keats's first night in the grave.
When I thought out my dream, it was some days
old, a cluster of half-rooms with Austrian blinds,
and no France; it was the hundredth birthday
of my name grandmother.

The Invalid's Echo

It was as if he put a thermometer
back in its holder without shaking it,
or snatched a cigarette out of my mouth
like a secret breath, the way he put
his finger on the rest, and we were disconnected.

The thinnest paper was an unbidden blue,
that had summoned him (it took five calls),
sitting behind a desk, waking him
prematurely, as a parent-poem,
out of an unfrightened, ten-year stretch
of love, for twenty minutes by an open window.

His foliage was unlike that of any other,
his sound was like nothing else, my ears
were never rested; I would have spent
the rest of my life felling his timber,
never taking my eyes off him,
always looking straight at his mouth,
if that was how he liked it.

He practises at death with each embrace;
in the language of our grandmothers,
who spoke God's name continually,
forgotten by our own free will,
he says a prayer for the dying over
himself and me; his endearments
execute the house's deepest reds.

A house heals easily, blood shed
in the past loses its hue; if I could die
the same death in the same air
as him, I would wish my grave
untended too, like everybody else's;

like the bulb that has not been washed
since the revolution, the hole
in the ceiling that has left
a little pile of plaster on the floor.

I think his family is so ancient,
his heart must still be over on the right,
though I have searched for it before
in full swing until it shrank to nothing,
merging with my name, that comes
from nowhere, and is ownerless,
like all we can see of the stars.

Now, like them, I lie with my back
to him, his chance neighbour,
watching the entrance to the house,
but not the house. The long autumn
has scattered its poisonous seeds,
so I will have no October child.

By the time I have the dream
that he will seek the word
with his fingers — the word that can
scarcely be used — that having forgotten
everything he will imagine the sky
in its second appearance as
the quintessence of blue,

I will be freezing in my short jacket.
In my last dream it was after January;
I was buying food for him when
a truck I have lost track of
came rattling into the overfulfilled courtyard.

The Man with Two Women

I'd been walking
                on a very old street
leading to the sea,
                    to a gritty beach
with huge stones,
                    where I would sit
in a stylish sundress,
                        laced boots and pearls,
re-reading five, ten times,
                        the simplest letters
from people who lived there
                        and emigrated.

It was a hopelessly
                    ill-advised summer,
one of a hundred
                bizarre days,
of lip-cutting wind
                and gold-enclosed
Irish clouds,
            rocking their past
in their arms as if
                they were still in their
army uniforms with
                the shoulder-tabs removed.

My tired skin
            was letting the rain
get inside the halves
                of my collar when
he entered as he
                would his own home,
placing himself
            there in the square

like a monument
                and suddenly,
in the doorway,
                pulling off his shirt.

Though I never promised
                my long kiss
to anyone,
                he turned his yard-wide
shoulders as if
                harnessed, like a
grand piano,
                suspended upside-
down, over
                my head.

I could have
                edged the breeze,
never within a house,
                to pour sand
into his mouth,
                but getting dark
is the world's fault:
                Send me
my winter.

Gigot Sleeves

There are bibles left about the house:
here is the bible open, here is the bible shut,
a spreading here, a condensation there.

The double-cherry performs a dance behind
triple gauze, she takes out the bulldogs,
masters a pistol, sleeps on a camp bed

without a fireplace or curtain, in the
narrow sliproom over the front hall —
a woman-sized, un-beringed, inexact fit.

When she hears the wheels of his carriage
she blows out the candle, she does not yearn
for the company of even a lamp.

For a gown-length, she chooses
a book-muslin patterned with lilac
thunder and lightning. Her skirts

are splashed with purple suns, the sleeves
set in as they used to be fifteen years
ago. If she takes up a piece of sewing,

she will be shirt-making; in a laundry-book
she writes as though fifteen hundred Englishmen
had been slaughtered just beyond the garden,

or it was there Trelawney threw the frankincense
and salt into the fire, poured the wine
and oil over the wave-worn depths of Shelley.

Her petticoats have neither curve nor wave
in them, the whole depth of the house,
like a secret tie between a wound and its weapon.

And everything is emaciated — the desk
on her knees, the square of carpet, the black
horsehair sofa — and the five-foot-seven by sixteen

inches, of a pair of months, stopped.

The Most Emily of All

When you dream wood I dream water.
When you dream boards, or cupboard,
I dream a lake of rain, a race sprung
from the sea. If you call out 'house' to me
and I answer 'library', you answer me
by the very terms of your asking,
as a sentence clings tighter
because it makes no sense.

Your light hat with the dark band
keeps turning up; you pull it right
down over your head and run the fingers
of your right hand up and down
in a groove on the door panel. A finger
going like this into my closed hand
feels how my line of life turns back
upon itself, in the kind of twilight
before the moon is seen.

A verse from a poem by Lermentov
continually goes round
in my head. A full ten days
has elapsed since I started my
'You can go or stay' letter, increasingly
without lips like the moon that night,
a repercussive mouth made for nothing,
and used for nothing.
Just let me moisten your dreamwork
with the lower half of the letter,
till my clove-brown eyes beget a taller blue.

No Streets, No Numbers

for Janice Fitzpatrick

The wind bruises the curtains' jay-blue stripes
like an unsold fruit or a child who writes
its first word. The rain tonight in my hair
runs a firm, unmuscular hand over something
sand-ribbed and troubled, a desolation
that could erase all memory of warmth
from the patch of vegetation where torchlight
has fallen. The thought that I might miss
even a second of real rain is like the simple
double knock of the stains of birth and death,
two men back to back carrying furniture
from a room on one side of the street
to a room on the other. And the weather
is a girl with woman's eyes like a knife-wound
in her head. Such is a woman's very deep
violation as a woman; not like talk,
not like footsteps; already a life crystallises
round it; and time, that is so often only a word,
'Later, later', spills year into year like three days'
post, or the drawing-room with the wall
pulled down.

I look into the endless settees
of the talk-dried drawing-room where all
the colours are wrong. Is that because
I unshaded all the lamps so their sunny,
unhurt movements would be the colour
of emotions which have no adventures?
But I'm afraid of the morning most,
which stands like a chance of life
on a shelf, or a ruby velvet dress,
cut to the middle of the back,
that can be held on the shoulder by a diamond lizard.

A stone is nearly a perfect secret, always
by itself, though it touches so much, shielding
its heart beyond its strong curtain of ribs
with its arm. Not that I want you
to tell me what you have not told anyone:
how your narrow house propped up window
after window, while the light sank and sank;
why your edges, though they shine,
no longer grip precisely like other people;
how sometimes the house won, and sometimes
the sea-coloured, sea-clear dress,
made new from one over a hundred years old,
that foamed away the true break
in the year, leaving the house
masterless and flagless. That dream
of a too early body undamaged
and beautiful, head smashed to pulp,
still grows in my breakfast cup;
it used up the sore red of the applebox,
it nibbled at the fortnight of our violent
Christmas like a centenarian fir tree.

I talk as if the evenings had been fine,
the roof of my shelves not broken
like an oath on crossed rods,
or I had not glimpsed myself
as the Ides of September, white
at the telephone. Two sounds
spin together and fight for sleep
between the bed and the floor,
an uneasy clicking-to of unsorted
dawn-blue plates, the friction
of a skirt of hands refusing to let go.
And how am I to break into
this other life, this small eyebrow,

six inches off mine, which has been
blown from my life like the most aerial
of birds? If the summer that never burnt,
and began two days ago, is ashes now,
autumn's backbone will have the pallor
of the snowdrop, the shape of the stone
showing in the wall. Our first summer-time
night, we will sit out drinking
on the pavement of Bird Street,
where we kissed in the snow, as the day
after a dream in which one really was
in love teases out the voice reserved for children.

Clotho

Music is my heroine, the synthetic kisses
of a woman's body. Drop by drop
she distilled them, I watched the non-togetherness
of her sweetish old-maid lips,
her trained and pocket-mouthed smile.

Like the shadow of an aeroplane
with but one side of wings,
she moved parallel to me,
leaving the air unflown.

My arms were stretched as high
and wide as they could go,
a distaff reaching from heaven to earth.
But there was nothing to burn
my tongue on, not even a broken stalk
of lilac-veined sound behind her broken eyes.

Blue does not describe them, they were
a blue and silver room
that sent me half-filled away.
I dropped three-quarters
of my words for I did not need them.

They should be another colour,
there should be black swans,
though a satellite is never
anything but feminine, and crawls
under your pillow
because of the horror of touch.

There should be a darkness
which is anything but death,
not the false daylight of the stage,

the most expensive white
of all those pairs of hands
born for a few sealed railway trains,
all of which were dead by morning.

In just these moments it has grown dark,
and the moon, the semi-human,
radioactive moon, is at a diagonal
past childbearing, neither lying down
nor sitting, since this
is a flowerless month.

I am possessed of such strength
that I knock down my servant,
my house god, my all-powerful
mistress of tone, and her moan
comes clear-cut from another world,
as if translating.

The Partners' Desk

Yesterday was a gift, a copy of the afternoon,
a heavily wrapped book, a rolled manuscript.
Its paper was buff with blue lines, the sheets
ragged at the top, and not quite legal size.
It was secured on three sides by green ribbons
like a wooden tongue of land or the leafy miles
of a ribbon-maker and, whether it was a letter
he withheld from me, I swore to seal it through death.

The colour is deep enough by itself to make
the children pray for the dead; it is a children's morning.
I arranged the Christmas tree in its green outfit,
producing its green against the grey sky like handwriting
that has been traced over or, when snow tires us,
the sunshine inside and out of my birthday dove.
Both our birthdays are today, and I was playing with
its feather on the bed as if it were a brake

on the thawing weather, that almost-summer
had already arrived. Being still in the grip
of a dream of pearls which robbed me
of my un-English language (yesterday
he dreamed of laburnums). It is his December,
though the wine is May's, and we should keep birds
only in winter, as we burn the winter
in our curse-laden, extinguished Christmas tree.

Everything I do passes through a narrow door,
and the door seems rather heavy. When I play
the piano my eyes turn brown; it is not a matter
of eyes, it is something darker than eye-colour,
and we are all part of it. When I teach the continents
to my favourite daughter, my father is there
though I do not see him. His mood is towards evening.
He asks the bird how many years he has to live,

or how long the hours will continue to strike.
How very deliberately the bird breaks off,
praising the stillness. He compares this cry
with his outward appearance, he strokes the veins
on the back of his left hand and extends
his fingers, he looks up at the ceiling
and down at the floor, he feels in his breast
pocket and pulls a green pamphlet out,

saying, 'The finest summer I can ever remember
produced you,' and I remember a second,
gentler dream, of my wedding year,
where we took a walk across loose stones,
and he took my hands and stretched them out
as if I were on a cross, but not being punished.
You know the renewed rousing of your fingers
in a dream, your hand glides through the air,

they are not fingers at all. He will leave me
the school clock, the partners' desk, the hanging
lamp, the head bearing the limbs, as I will leave her
the moonphase watch and the bud vase. I restart
my diary and reconstruct the days. I look upon
the life-bringing cloud as cardboard
and no reason for the life of another soul, yet still
today is the true midsummer day.

The War Ending

In the still world
between the covers of a book,
silk glides through your name
like a bee sleeping in a flower
or a seal that turns its head to look
at a boy rowing a boat.

The fluttering motion of your hands
down your body presses into my thoughts
as an enormous broken wave,
a rainbow or a painting being torn
within me. I remove the hand
and order it to leave.

Your passion for light
is so exactly placed,
I read them as eyes, mouth, nostrils,
disappearing back into their mystery
like the war that has gone
into us ending;

there you have my head,
a meeting of Irish eyes
with something English:
and now,
today,
it bursts.

Breaking the Blue

Deluged with the dustless air, unspeaking likeness:
you, who were the spaces between words in the act of reading,
a colour sewn on to colour, break the blue.

Single version of my mind deflected off my body,
side-altar, sacramental, tasting-table, leaf to my
emptying shell, heart with its aortic opening,

your mouth, my dress was the scene that framed
your shut eye like hands or hair, we coiled
in the lifelong snake of sleep, we poised together

against the crevice formed by death's forefinger
and thumb, where her shoulder splits when desire
goes further than the sender will allow.

Womb-encased and ever-present mystery without
release, your even-coloured foliage seems a town garden
to my inaccessible, severely mineral world.

Fragments of once-achieved meaning, ready to leave
the flesh, re-integrate as lover, mother, words
that overwhelm me: You utter, become music, are played.

She Which Is Not, He Which Is

An elm box without any shape inscribed
like a tool in the closed vessel of the world;
I will be flat like a dream on both sides,
or a road that makes one want to walk.

My words will be without words
like a net hidden in a lake,
their pale individual moisture.
My eyes will not be the eyes of a poet
whose voice is beyond death;
this face, these clothes, will be a field in autumn
and the following autumn, will be two sounds,
the second of which is deeper.

The sky for me on any one night
will be the successive skies over the course
of a year, for time that I love
will have cut up and entered my body;
time will have gathered the roots
of my last spring, floating rather
than anchored, and thrust them between
the two planes of my cheek and brow.

Even now, his lips are becoming
narrower and bloodless, ever-searching,
razor-like; unforgettable time,
during which I forget time, a new sort
of time that descends so far down
into me and still stays pure.

I imagine his house as a possible setting
for the harmony between one drop of water
and another, one wave and another wave,
where the light accustoms one to light
and each occurrence is a touch.

When we pass through some darkness
the waiting has pulled us.
Without the help of words, words take place.

Compared with this absence, weighed,
diluted in time, presence is abandonment,
absence his manner of appearing,
as though one received from outside
the energy to accept the swept room
as much as the sweeping.

Though each instant of light
wipes away a little of it,
we shall not lose the way
in which things receive it:

Carry me who am death
like a bowl of water
filled to the brim
from one place to another.

The Snow Speaker

So little of the earth, you
open the earth for me.

Having no more need of me
than I of you,
I am as alone with you
as without you.

I try to love the sky
as the sea's accomplice,
but nothing human
can help us know the stars.

Threshing a poem
or a grape-harvest
takes four equal limbs
and a horizontal cutting
that has always already begun.

You are speaking of
that wholly woven day,
not stunning, nor bitter.

Your pleasure just fits
on the postcard of evening;
an envelope would have given off
too sharp a smell.

Another room closes
the door of the sun
and gathers carefully
all the water that falls.

Marconi's Cottage

Small and watchful as a lighthouse,
a pure clear place of no particular childhood,
it is as if the sea had spoken in you
and then the words had dried.

Bitten and fostered by the sea
and by the British spring,
there seems only this one way of happening,
and a poem to prove it has happened.

Now I am close enough, I open my arms
to your castle-thick walls, I must learn
to use your wildness when I lock and unlock
your door weaker than kisses.

Maybe you are a god of sorts,
or a human star, lasting in spite of us
like a note propped against a bowl of flowers,
or a red shirt to wear against light blue.

The bed of your mind has weathered
books of love, you are all I have gathered
to me of otherness; the worn glisten
of your flesh is relearned and reloved.

Another unstructured, unmarried, unfinished
summer, slips its unclenched weather
into my winter poems, cheating time
and blood of their timelessness.

Let me have you for what we call
forever, the deeper opposite of a picture,
your leaves, the part of you
that the sea first talked to.

On Her Second Birthday

for Emer Mary Charlotte Rose

In the beginning I was no more
than a rising and falling mist
you could see through without seeing.

A flame burnt up the paper
on which my gold was written,
the wind like a soul
seeking to be born
carried off half
of what I was able to say.

It seems as though
to explain the shape of the world
we must fall apart,
throw ourselves upon the world,
slip away from ourselves
through the world's inner road,
whose atoms make us weary.

Suddenly ever more lost
between the trees
I saw the edge of the forest
which had no end,
which I came dangerously close
to accepting for my life,

and followed with my eye a shadow
floating from horizon to horizon
which I mistook for my own.
It grew greater while I grew less,
gliding like a world, a tapestry
one looks at from the back.

The more it changed
the more it changed me into itself,
till I regarded it as more real
than all else, more ardent
than love. Higher than the air
of a dream,
a field in which I ripened
from an unmoving, continually nascent
light into pure light.

My contours can still
just be made out, in the areas of fragrance
of its power over me.
A slight tremor betrays
the imperfection of the union
in its first surface.

But I flow outwards till I am something
belonging to it and flower again
more perfectly everywhere present in it.
It believes in me,
it cannot do without me,
I know its name:
one day it will pass my mind into its body.

Candles at Three Thirty

The year fades without ripening,
but glitters as it withers
like an orange stuck with cloves
or Christmas clouds.

Bits of very new,
dream-quilted sky
are touched to an arrangement,
all but kiss.

Dark blue gathers around the waist
into a humbler colour;
two cottages flush with the road
slowly edge back.

When I am all harbour, ask too much,
go up like the land
to points and precipices,
meanwhile is my anchor.

The island with its quick primrose light
turns aside and walks away
from my swollen shadows,
but carries the road southwards.

Frail as tobacco flowers,
a featherweight seagull
still damp on my brocade curtain
is ready for sea again.

A meaningless white thread
of pale travel-sleep
rippling one side only
of his unlighted eyes,

intelligent and soulless,
sees everybody happening
as down a warmed room.
The upper half of the house made fast,

we try to batten the door-windows,
but one won't fasten,
the thin edge of the sea's blade
curves around its oak, rustless as flesh.

Out between the rosemary hedges,
sky and sea part in a long
mauve-silver tress
like an oyster shell

that has held life between its lips
so long,
it seems so long
since life left it wrecked there.

Winter's frosty standstill
will just leave the lips clear
as on a bridge
of would-be sunshine.

But now the intensification
of light in the lower sky
like a stairway outside
the side of a house

acts directly on the blood,
not the mind, to make the sea
appear more light than water,
familiar as a fireside.

Field Heart

If I had dipped the tip of my finger
in water to cool your tongue,
you would have tasted salt off trees
forty miles from the sea.

Our voices in ordinary conversation
floated between farmhouses:
the pilot-light of a candle
burned in the open air
with no attempt to flicker.

Firmly-knit thatch
simply rested on the eaves
of its own permeable weight.
Slowly and steadily, the storm
that shared your name
reduced its current,
till every attentively incomprehending
tile of your skin
caught and flamed.

Nothing was to be seen through the closed lids
of your eventful dreaming,
the closed avenue of your new senses
beginning as absolute strangers
their ready-to-be-reaped, matured homecoming.

Through some friction with material substance,
like engaging a clutch, or intermeshing gears,
you turned the dew into something enchanted,
unbolted, a collapsible telescope,
a balloon untethered, a ball
from which the air has escaped.

You were now inside a lift
rising between two floors, no longer noticeable,
being whipped like the cork of a champagne bottle
out through a dark and narrow shaft
or rushing valley, into a higher frequency,
a faster vibration — into all the Irelands!

Bring your loosened soul near,
look through,
meet my day-consciousness
in the lawfulness of what is living:
return a different June to me —
once only, slide
until the union holds.

Elegy for an Irish Speaker

Numbered day,
night only just beginning,
be born very slowly, stay
with me, impossible to name.

Do I know you, Miss Death,
by your warrant, your heroine's head
pinned against my hero's shoulder?
The seraphim are as cold
to each other in Paradise:
and the room of a dying man
is open to everyone.
The knitting together of your two spines
is another woman
reminding of a wife, his life
surrounds you as a sun,
consumes your light.

Are you waiting to be fertilized,
dynamic death, by his dark company?
To be warmed in your wretched
overnight lodgings
by his kind words and small talk
and powerful movements?
He breaks away from your womb
to talk to me,
he speaks so with my consciousness
and not with words, he's in danger
of becoming a poetess.

Roaming root of multiple meanings,
he shouts himself out
in your narrow amphora,
your tasteless, because immortal, wine.
The instant of recognition

is unsweet to him, scarecrow word
sealed up, second half
of a poetic simile lost somewhere.

Most foreign and cherished reader,
I cannot live without
your trans-sense language,
the living furrow of your spoken words
that plough up time.
Instead of the real past
with its deep roots,
I have yesterday,
I have minutes when
you burn up the past
with your raspberry-coloured farewell
that shears the air. Bypassing
everything, even your frozen body,
with your full death, the no-road-back
of your speaking flesh.

The Aisling Hat

October — you took away my biography —
I am grateful to you, you offer me gifts
for which I have still no need.

I search for a lost, unknown song
in a street as long as a night,
stamped with my own surname.

A spy-glass at the end of it,
a cool tunnel crushed by binoculars
into your grandfather's house.

The elegant structure of the heart
is a net cast over everything in sight,
its lace design of perforations, truancy.

Over your face a cognac eagleskin
was tightly stretched, my cart-horse,
dray-horse, drew your heavy chariot

chasing after time you beat aloud
which had already vanished into overtones:
you were his co-discoverer, his museum,

his clock of coal, clock of limestone,
shale or schist, his mountain top
sculpted into a foal, his warm pitcher.

Even your least movement was connected
with the very composition of the soil,
you lived and died according to its laws.

Your Promethean head radiated
ash-blue quartz, your blue-black hair
some feathered, Paleolithic arrowhead,

set off the bold strokes of your ungainly
arms, created for handshakes, sliding
like the knight's move, to the side.

You were intoxicated like a woman
caressed with the lips alone
by the noise of your thousand breaths.

You felt nauseated, like a pregnant
woman, a rose inscribed in stone,
unread newspapers clattered in your hands.

Your horse-sweat was the poetry
of collective breathing, your urine-colour
the sense of the start of a race.

Your eyebrows arched like a composer's,
an accordion of wrinkles repaired
the fluids of your forehead, then drew apart.

Your powerful thorax gave velvet-
throated orders, there was a married charm
in your nuptial animation floating forward

to sow itself in the arid
frontier atmosphere. Your skin changed
to an absolute courtesy

but never ceased dreaming;
seeds of laughter pierced your chest
that now lies ensconced in the velvet.

Broken sign of the unbroken continuum,
you fused into a single thread,
time fed you with lightnings and downpours

so you rained hushing sounds,
while river air hovered over the room
and sucked in a crescent of the sea.

You sharpened yourself like a pencil
in the tender midwife of your shell,
in your geometric giddiness.

Your golden hands like hills
of tired rags stirred up the dust,
flushed horseman, streaked feldspar.

There was fire in your hands, blisters
on your palms as if you had been rowing,
heavy fire in your naked eyes

monkish in their furious, yellowish
glitter, still and sensual the shining
points of your equine eyes.

Twin wings unseverable
were those enormous eyes, legs of the heron
reconciled to their uselessness.

Neck of the swan theatrically
open, ripping off the days due to you,
expressing your allegiance.

A noose around the icy place
from which flowed your consciousness
like mineral-water cheeriness.

The earth like some great brown
ceiling came rushing at your head.
No one heard it hiss in the shadows.

Roses which must have been cut
in the morning stood exchanging lights,
as your phonetic light turned off

and the lips of your fireproof eye
burned like poppies, firmly reminding
everyone that speech is work.

Until we remembered that to speak
is to be forever on the road,
listening for the foreigner's footstep.

I felt a shiver of novelty
as if someone had summoned you
by name, to the most beautiful applause.

Your eye raised the picture
to its own level, you retreated
into the picture before my eyes

like hello or goodbye;
I got tangled up in it
as in a robe ready to be woven

from a soft *L* and a short aspiration,
or the most recent barbaric layer
the bark of linden peels off itself.

Woodcutting tuned you, absorptive
and resorptive, to an entire segmented
lemon grove of fatigue and secret energy.

You burst the frontier at some
undefended silk crack — shreds
of splashed brain on the chestnut trees.

Now all questions and answers rotate about —
did it thunder or not? Now I begin
the second stage of restoring the picture.

The helix of my ear takes on new whorls,
becomes a bittersweet instrument,
to undress spring from the neurotic May,

the inherited river, the world
which, unpopulated, continues
to signal his speech-preparatory moves.

He does not resemble a man
waiting for a rendezvous.
The area he covers in his stroll

is too large, he is still
a stranger there, until his storm matures,
and what might have been alive, knowledge-bearing.

His body is unwashed, his beard
wild, his fingernails broken,
his ears deaf from the silence.

Carefree skater on air, his language
cannot be worn down, though I
avoid it in my feebleness.

He controls my hair, my fingernails,
he swallows my saliva, so accustomed
is he to the thought that I am here.

I need to get to know his bones,
the deep sea origins of the mountains,
the capsule of his crypt,

how life below starts to play
with phosphorus and magnesium.
How cancelled benevolence gains a script

from a departure so in keeping
with its own structure — his denial
of history's death, by the birth of his storm.

The Albert Chain

Like an accomplished terrorist, the fruit hangs
from the end of a dead stem, under a tree
riddled with holes like a sieve. Breath smelling
of cinnamon retires into its dream to die there.
Fresh air blows in, morning breaks, then the mists
close in; a rivulet of burning air
pumps up the cinders from their roots,
but will not straighten in two radiant months
the twisted forest. Warm as a stable,
close to the surface of my mind,
the wild cat lies in the suppleness of life,
half-stripped of its skin, and in the square
beyond, a squirrel stoned to death
has come to rest on a lime tree.

I am going back into war, like a house
I knew when I was young: I am inside,
a thin sunshine, a night within a night,
getting used to the chalk and clay and bats
swarming in the roof. Like a dead man
attached to the soil which covers him,
I have fallen where no judgment can touch me,
its discoloured rubble has swallowed me up.
For ever and ever, I go back into myself:
I was born in little pieces, like specks of dust,
only an eye that looks in all directions can see me.
I am learning my country all over again,
how every inch of soil has been paid for
by the life of a man, the funerals of the poor.

I met someone I believed to be on the side
of the butchers, who said with tears, 'This
is too much.' I saw you nailed to a dry rock,
drawing after you under the earth the blue fringe
of the sea, and you cried out 'Don't move!'

as if you were already damned. You are muzzled
and muted, like a cannon improvised from an iron
pipe. You write to me generally at nightfall,
careful of your hands, bruised against bars:
already, in the prime of life, you belong
to the history of my country, incapable
in this summer of treason, of deliberate treason,
charming death away with the rhythm of your arm.

As if one part of you were coming to the rescue
of the other, across the highest part of the sky,
in your memory of the straight road flying past,
I uncovered your feet as a small refuge,
damp as winter kisses in the street,
or frost-voluptuous cider over
a fire of cuttings from the vine.
Whoever goes near you is isolated
by a double row of candles. I could escape
from any other prison but my own
unjust pursuit of justice
that turns one sort of poetry into another.

Lines for Thanksgiving

Two floors, their invisible staircase
crouching muscularly,
an old wall, unusually high,
interwoven like the materials for a nest,
the airtight sensation of slates:
all as gracefully apart
as a calvary from a crib
or the woman born in my sleep
from the stranger me that is satisfied
by any street with the solemn name of a saint.

The moon there, fuller than any other,
slips through my fingers into every fold
of the sky in turn, stirring up satin
like a mother roughing a boy's hair.
Eternally repeating its double journey
and the same message, as if it were
still impossible to speak
from one town to the next.

The fire keeping in all night
is an extra gas jet, its several
thicknesses unequal in length
like the rays of a monstrance.
If I had just won a victory
it was over everything that was not
myself, by the water's edge.

Captain Lavender

Night-hours. The edge of a fuller moon
waits among the interlocking patterns
of a flier's sky.

Sperm names, ovum names, push inside
each other. We are half-taught
our real names, from other lives.

Emphasise your eyes. Be my flare-
path, my uncold begetter,
my air-minded bird-sense.

The War Degree

You smell of time as a Bible smells of thumbs,
a bank of earth alive with mahogany-coloured
flowers — not time elaborately thrown away,
(you wound yourself so thoroughly into life),
but time outside of time, new pain, new secret,
that I must re-fall in love with the shadow
of your soul, drumming at the back of my skull.

Tonight, when the treaty moves all tongues,
I want to take the night out of you,
the sweet Irish tongue in which
death spoke and happiness wrote:

a wartime, heart-stained autumn drove
fierce half-bricks into the hedges; tree-muffled
streets vanished in the lack of news.
Like a transfusion made direct from arm
to arm, birds call uselessly to each other
in the sub-acid, wintry present. The pursed-up
fragrances of self-fertile herbs
hug defeat like a very future lover.

Now it is my name and not my number
that is nobody now, walking on a demolished
floor, where dreams have no moral.
And the door-kiss is night meeting night.

Editors' Note

These poems appear, sometimes in different forms, in the following collections: pages 13-29, *The Flower Master and Other Poems* (The Gallery Press, 1993; original edition, *The Flower Master*, Oxford University Press, 1982); pages 30-38, *Venus and the Rain* (Gallery, revised edition, 1994; OUP, 1984); pages 39-51, *On Ballycastle Beach* (OUP, 1988; Wake Forest University Press, 1988; Gallery, with revisions, 1995). 'The Bond' appeared originally in *Pharaoh's Daughter*, poems by Nuala Ní Dhomhnaill, with translations into English (Gallery, 1990; WFUP, 1993). The poems on pages 53-75 appear in slightly different forms in *Marconi's Cottage* (Gallery, 1991; WFUP, 1992) and on pages 76-92 in *Captain Lavender* (Gallery, 1994; WFUP, 1995).

The Gallery Press and Wake Forest University Press will publish Medbh McGuckian's sixth collection of poems in 1998.

Peter Fallon and Dillon Johnston